D1712012

# Spool of Thread

by Rogene Lee Jados

TO SOW THE FALLOW SOIL

**Winston-Derek Publishers, Inc.**
Pennywell Drive—Post Office Box 90883
Nashville, Tennessee 37209

First printing

PUBLISHED BY WINSTON-DEREK PUBLISHERS
Nashville, Tennessee 37205

Library of Congress Catalog Card No: 85-51407
ISBN 938232-91-6

Printed in the United States of America

I dedicate this book to my husband, Leon, whose love
gives me wings.

## *Foreword*

I like to compare my life to a spool of thread. Each time I break off a piece of thread to mend a tear in a garment, or use a much larger piece to make a quilt, each piece of thread is a part of the whole spool. My life is comprised of small vignettes, happenings, joyful moments, nature that has touched my soul, and also sadness. I've grown as a person because of everything in my life that I have experienced. If we use each piece of life(thread) fully our lives will attain a peace and joy far beyond what we might imagine.

# Table of Contents

A spool of thread
needles and pins
I spin my threads
of life;
with faith
laughter
and a love for all God's
creatures
who have taught me
kindness
gentleness
and an indescribable sense
of God's goodness

Our highest assurance of the goodness
of Providence seems to me to rest in
the flowers, our desires, our food, are all
really necessary for our existence in
the first instance. But this rose is
an extra. Its smell and its colour
are an embellishment of life, not a
condition of it. It is only goodness
which gives extras, and so I say again
that we have much to hope from the flowers.

Sir Arthur Conan Doyle
Sherlock Holmes

# A Lesson from Mourning Doves

I feel very honored. A pair of Mourning Doves have built a nest in a large spruce tree in my spring garden. It's an exquisite setting with the daffodils, tulips, wild trillium and periwinkle in bloom.

The honeysuckle and lilac are budding out and will be in full bloom in a few days. To me it looks like a view of heaven as I watch the beautiful Mourning Doves light on the spruce tree, taking turns setting on their eggs.

My heart feels a wave of peace. I thank God for this little niche, a small corner of the world for me to enjoy. The Mourning Doves trust me, and as I sit on the porch and sip my cup of tea I feel honored because of their trust.

Instinctively they sense that I will not harm them or their unhatched babies.

They weave their particular thread of life, by taking turns setting on their eggs, flying off searching for food or standing guard duty. What loyalty and devotion they have for each other. It must get boring and uncomfortable sitting on their nest hour after hour, yet they maintain their responsibility with such casual dignity. Whatever the weather, I hear them singing their mournful call. It's as soothing as love words spoken in a whisper.

The ritual the Mourning Doves maintain has helped me. I have watched their patience and devotion and thought of the many times that I have failed to express my love and devotion.

I feel humbled because I have seen myself fall short in patience, and the Mourning Doves patience seems endless. If only I can learn to be as diligent in my responsibilities as they are. I feel ashamed, but hopeful, because by my feelings I know I have already learned from them.

Soon they will leave their nest in the spruce tree. I will miss them for they have brought something special to this spring. I'm thankful that they honored me with their presence.

As they weave their thread of life I will have the empty nest to remind me of the continuity of life, and next year, who knows, maybe they will welcome spring with me once again.

## *Kindness Is Contagious*

As we approached the Great Smoky Mountain National Park and I viewed the panoramic scene, I thought; nothing can be more beautiful than this . . . nothing! How naive!

We entered the park and drove down a two track road zigzagging thru the mountains following the bank of a mountain creek. I marveled at the boulders of every size that lie in nature's pattern and at the changing color of the water blending with shade and sun. The giant trees and tiny delicate flowers complete the exquisite scene.

The Smoky Mountians are breathtaking from a distance, but you haven't seen their beauty until you've sat in their lap.

I remember sitting in my gramma's lap. The warmth of her body, her special smell, and every line in her beautiful face. The twinkle in her eyes a signal that what she was telling me was make-believe.

It made me reflect on how we view people—first impressions—snap judgements—someone else's opinion. Jesus always looked beneath the surface and saw the goodness in everyone he touched.

If we look beyond human frailties we will find goodness in everyone we touch, and more importantly we will find kindness flowing from us that is contagious.

# *Look, Look Around You*

As I gaze out the window into my backyard at the glorious autumn colors they hold the promise of spring for me, more than the reality of winter. The colors of the leaves with the sun shining brightly on them is indescribable. Soon the leaves will be gone from the trees.

I will have a stark view of the pasture and surrounding woods. The deer are feeding in the pasture as they do every fall. I peek between the trees to catch a glimpse at these beautiful creatures.

They look up once in a while and gaze back at me. The deer make me think of the coming winter. I say a little prayer in hopes that the winter isn't too hard on them. I look forward to winter.

I know I'm in the minority in my feelings, but I love the fires in the fireplace, cuddled up in a chair with my knitting listening to the sound of the wind. When the winds are mild they are as soothing as the purring of a cat. The loud gale winds of winter make me very nervous. I don't know why.

My husband and I both have the same reaction a foreboding of something about to happen.

I've tried to reason it out maybe the power and strength of the wind scares me, or is it something deep in my being, an instinct that tells me what could happen, and did many years ago, to people who could not find shelter from the freezing winds.

I feel very happy and thankful for the warm house and fire.

Each autumn seems more beautiful than the one before, I keep thinking of spring. It's as if God is saying, "Look, look around you."

The scene is so vibrant and its promise is so clear. Even when the leaves are scattered on the ground like a multicolored quilt covering the grass and every niche and crevice around my home, I feel the promise of spring. Could this be why God made autumn so beautiful?

No other time of the year is as lovely or such a contrast to the stark beauty of winter. Let's enjoy the beauty of fall, collect lovely pictures and store them in a drawer in our mind to be pulled out whenever we need them.

What a blessing we have in using our mind as a storeroom for memories of things past and to hold pictures once again in our hands: Autumn . . . God's lovely lavishly wrapped early Christmas present . . . enjoy!

# God's Greatest Cathedral

O Lord, I love the beauty of your house, the dwelling place of your Glory. I find myself whispering this litany of praise often when I'm in God's greatest Cathedral . . . the outdoors.

The serene stillness of the night, the beauty of the pine trees heavy with scent surround me.

The whippoorwill and frogs fill the air with their chorus of songs that put the finest choir to shame.

Understandably, as a child I found myself busy chasing butterflies, or watching birds in flight. I was too young to appreciate the smell of the air after a spring rain.

Now I find myself drinking in the sweet smell of spring until I feel my lungs will burst.

The older I get the more magnified my sense of appreciating nature becomes.

I delight in watching the chipmunks play and chatter to each other, or watch the Baltimore Orioles and Scarlet Tanagers taking turns bathing in the birdbath. Their singing, splashing and fighting for their turn is like children frolicking in a swimming pool.

Whatever the reason is for our clearer insight as we mature I'm thankful to be a part of it. My front porch has become my haven to watch rabbits hop leisurely across my lawn, stopping here and there to nibble at the clover.

What a tender gentle animal they are, so trusting and vulnerable to predators. I worry about them almost as if they are my children. Their threads of life are very fragile—but then I think of how they blend in with the changes of the seasons, most animals have this protection, and it quiets my fears.

They have accepted God's plan for them trusting joyfully in each new day. I have learned much from my outdoor friends.

7

# Old People Are Like the Evening of the Day

I love my antique furniture and what-nots for the character they have acquired over their lives. As I dust and polish I like to imagine the former owners and the houses they were in.

The satiny patina of the furniture attests to the loving care each piece received. My eyes roam to the rocker in the corner. It's idle now, with an afghan thrown over the back and two rag dolls sitting helter skelter on it, but I imagine the swift scared rocking fretting over a sick child, or the companionable rocking of sewing and sharing with a friend, or rocking, cuddling and singing to a warm sleepy baby. I feel like the most recent link in the chain of their historical lives.

I love old people for the wonderful character they portray, too. Their strength and courage must come from their years of experience in life.

An old person with a stroke may not be able to remember what he did yesterday or a week ago, but he has the treasured memories of being a child.

He remembers roller-skating a hundred miles an hour, at least it seems like that when you're eight years old, or climbing a big high tree giving his loud Tarzan yell, scared cause he's so high off the ground, but what a thrilling scariness . . . I can't fall!

Old people derive so much comfort from these childhood recollections. I believe we revert back in time as a gift from God. It lets us once again run with the wind, relive the first fish we ever caught, lets us ride our bike one more time. Our mind and our imagination, what marvelous gifts.

Old people are tuned to the true values of life. From experience they have learned to flow with life's tide to enjoy a hug from a child, a walk with their pet. The thread of life weaves its spell and old people accept, understand, and let the rest be so much chaff.

The parallel I feel between my antique treasures and old people is old people are survivors, strong in spirit, so endearing.

My antiques have endured a continuity of existence that gives them a strength. I love the secrets they hide and their lasting beauty.

I feel blessed in my love for old people. They are like the evening of the day, my favorite time: Quiet stillness, beautiful sunsets, twinkling stars . . . Yes! Twinkling stars.

## *So Much Beauty to Enjoy*

I've been spending much of my summer on the golf course taking lessons in humility and patience—two of the privileges that are part of the game of golf.

I can't think of a better place to learn these valuable traits and also enjoy the lush beauty of nature.

The smell of fresh cut grass mingled with the breezes off Lake Michigan tempts me to breath deeply and drink in the fragrance of summer.

No wonder it's so difficult to keep my mind and eye on hitting a little white ball. My human frailties are so very obvious as I try to make my body do things my mind (imagination) has talked me into thinking I can do.

I feel very blessed and thankful for this hobby, to enjoy the beauty of nature with good friends who laugh and share my fun.

Our Lord gave us so much beauty to enjoy. He understands our needs and taking time to enjoy life is just as important and rewarding as the work we must do.

I whisper a silent litany of prayer to our Lord as I play my game of golf. His answer cames back loud and clear . . . Enjoy!

# God Whispers to Me
## Through Nature's Beauty

My long invigorating walks are not only good for my body and spirit; I also take my mind out for an airing.

My thoughts race up to the clouds, to the tops of the trees, gliding with the seagulls as they fly by, and drifting on the jet stream.

I file ideas, inspirations, random thoughts into my filing cabinet mind to be pulled out later.

When I return home you'd imagine my thoughts would be fuzzy and vague with cobwebs from my summer daydreams, but like the wild seeds drifting on the wind some fall and take root and grow in my mind. I long to share them.

White billowy sheer curtains—new fallen snow drifted into beautiful sculptured shapes and forms—white lace wedding gowns—a string of satiny white pearls—milk poured into a crystal glass—a glowing white candle on an altar—a drifting feathery white cloud—fresh white sheets with the smell of spring—milk glass dishes—white roses and wild trillium—snow white hair—crisp soda crackers—white shiny teeth complimenting a warm friendly smile—a garden of dancing lily of the valley, the scent surrounds my home and drifts inside on a gentle spring breeze—the angelic beauty of the baby girl wearing a frilly white night-gown—thick white fog makes me feel isolated, safe, and island alone—flying at 37,000 feet surrounded by snowy white clouds I'm held safely in God's open hand—white birch trees in a swamp stand elegantly like dancers on a stage.

All around me I see God's gift of beauty. It nourishes my faith. God whispers to me through the beauty of nature. May I always listen.

## *Dusting Out the Attic*

The air is rich with the delicious pungent smells of the autumn harvest. Nature was putting on its Mexican fiesta letting us know that fall had arrived. A summer fireworks display with splashes of vivid colors to oh! and ah! over.

I stop on my walk to enjoy the glorious fall scene. I watch the wild geese gliding on the lake. They stop to rest, feed and re-group for the long flight south. What beautiful elegant creatures they are. I find it difficult to take my eyes off of them and continue my walk.

My dog scampering on ahead of me turns around and impatiently looks at me as if to say, "come on slowpoke you promised me a long walk." Her mind is on chasing chipmunks that tease her unmercifully with their shrill squeals, and then they run for cover. I laugh at their fun and games.

My time alone, walking, contemplating and enjoying the changing season makes me feel shiny and new. I've cleaned out the worries stored in the attic of my mind. I've let them disappear like skipping stones tossed on the lake. I've dusted myself off and I'm ready to start anew.

# A Wild Flower and Me

Sometimes I like to play a guessing game, you pick a plant or animal that you might like to be.

My first choice would be a wild flower called Queen Anne's Lace. Its flowers when in bloom are a lovely lacy design crocheted by the hand of God. Some call it wild carrot, a lowly garden weed. I'd heard it called that many times as a child.

My job as a child was the weeding. When I pulled the Queen Anne's Lace (wild carrot) out of the garden, I marveled at the strong roots that reached deep into the soil, and yet its stems and flowers were fragile as they bent with the wind.

I also have strong roots inherited from my ancestors. Strong surviving roots that reach deep into my being . . . a mooring. Our ancestors give us a stability and security . . . our roots.

A field of wild flowers is a joy to behold and the lovely Queen Anne's Lace bending and dancing with the wind is a free spirit.

I admire this because I cherish my own freedom. My freedom is free will, a gift from our Lord. We decide with no strings attached what we will do with our lives.

God loves us very much and by giving us free will he's saying "Come follow me," but the choice is yours.

Maybe this guessing game isn't as silly as it seems. Not if it makes us reflect on the beauty of God's creation and more importantly look inside ourselves.

# The Empty Nest

All winter long I've observed a bird nest, perched on the top branch of a birch tree in my front yard. The vicious winter winds have scattered leaves and twigs all over the yard. On days when we have had blizzard conditions and fifty m.p.h. winds, I expected the nest to surely fall. It looks so fragile woven of nature's debris. The birds that built the nest using their architectural instincts really did a great job.

This was to be their home a cradle to rock their babies. It has served them well, as testament the empty nest in the middle of March.

It's a beautiful spring like day, melting snow, tiny riverlets of running water washing the earth's face. I look again at the empty nest in the leafless birch tree. It delights me! It has taken everything Old Man Winter could dish out and survived. The strong survivor in me chuckles—so have I!!!

# The Old Attain a Peace
# We Hunger For

Have you ever watched a river on a warm lazy summer day? So still and quiet smooth as silk, but jump in that same river for a swim.

You're in for a surprise as you feel the strength and power of the undercurrent not visible on the surface, but it's always there and will be as long as the river endures.

I think this very clearly describes a woman's nature so gentle, a soft tenderness. You can see it in the way she treats the man she loves, in the way she touches and handles her children.

So much her nature but let something threaten her child or loved one and a woman will draw on a strength and courage that isn't at all visible in her nature that she shows to the world, but without blinking an eye she would die for her child or loved one.

A man has this same strength and courageous nature but it's always out in the open, a very visible part of his make up. He may have a tender gentle side also, but it would never be mistaken or compared with a woman's presence.

I think we should be proud of the difference in a man's and woman's natural instinctive qualities. It's so right; so a part of the threads of life. We have these instinctive qualities that are similar but also very separate and different.

Just as animals' instincts are so different from each other. We should cherish these differences because a woman and man need to draw on these qualities from each other.

The expressive qualities in an old woman's eyes overwhelms me. They're just fabulous, rich with wisdom. Sometimes I'm scared to look into them. I feel they know me so well.

They've been through everything I have and so much more. I've always loved old people and to be in their company is such a joy.

They are so honest and speak with such basic good sense and always interjected somewhere is a childlike sense of humor so honest and truthful.

15

Old people seem to express this same anticipation as they near the end of their road in life. No fear but a quiet sense of peace and joy of anticipating going home.

When I have been on a vacation, I always enjoy it tremendously and I have such fun; but when I come back home and drive down our road and turn into the driveway, I feel a wave of peace and thankfulness. I'm home.

Old people have this peace. It is a growing living process that takes a lifetime to attain. When we attain this peace, it is the peace we have hungered for all our lives.

My father-in-law had this peace and strength that I greatly admired.

Every year he would say, "If I live until spring, I think I'll get a few chickens and rabbits to raise, and I think I'll plant a little garden." I'd laugh about it because I'd hear this every year.

The quiet gentle peace of accepting the thread of life (whatever will be) but yet the hope was there. he wanted to go on and was planning and looking ahead.

What a wonderful example he was to all of us; We all need this hope. This planning ahead.

## *The Warm Flow*

The warm flow of love is at the core of every relationship forever nourishing us. Like the warm flow of blood is always returning to our heart, love too returns full circle, heart touching heart.

## A Thirst for Love

I need to care for people
to be able to give love
It's like an unquenchable
thirst in me
It makes me feel alive, happy

Is this selfish?
this mother hen
clucking inside me
to the depths of my being

I want to love
It's when I'm happiest
Let me love you

# Safe, Warm, and Oh! So Loved

Sitting in a high wingback chair
makes me feel
like someone I love
is hugging me
A home feels like that too
cozy, warm, snug
wrapping its walls around you

# A Cradle of Love

Before I was born
you nourished me
I was cradled in your arms
as your arms
encircled
your ever expanding abdomen
I felt love!
your love

The shirts didn't really need pressing
or
the socks paired and rolled in a ball
Towels lined the shelves like soldiers
love wrapped in every fold
These things were done out of habit
a part of her daily routine
small tasks
part of a woman's work
satisfying a woman's need
The best part of loving
is
giving, giving, giving

## With Echoes of Love

Dad, I wonder if you know
how much you have done
to make me the woman
I have become;
You held my hand
as the dentist
pulled my first tooth
You talked to the thunder
and lightning
calming my fears
You said NO
with a firm finality
resounding with echoes of love
You let me walk away
strong and sure
of my own worth
Dad, I love you
and though I'm a woman now
I'll always need your love

# *Friendship and Unconditional Love*

There's nothing more comfortable
than good friends
or an old pair of shoes
An old pair of shoes
has adjusted
to all of your imperfections
and good friends
love you in spite of them

I've hurt someone I love
when will I learn
to stop judging people
by not judging
we express a great kindness
and love
Only by living through
experiences good or bad
can we make choices
Choices that are right for us
The experiences of living
are like the roots of a plant
feeding
helping us to grow and bloom
forgive me, my dear friend

## Love Sparkles Like A Diamond

The diamond sparkles beaming signals of love
back to me
the diamond you gave to me
so long ago
A symbol of your love is still shining brightly
like our love
Its beauty is reflected in my love for you

Soon after we met
I knew you were the—one
We could talk for hours
and never touch
I knew I'd found
a part of me
and
when we touched
I touched a star
—our star

Ten times three plus seven more
counting my happiness
I add up the score
Please, dear God
keep him safe for me
for with out his love
there would be no—me

My happiness is encompassed in your smile
and a wink from across the room
has my heart doing somersaults
and beating with a strange happy beat
Is this love?
maybe
One thing I'm sure of;
this is a beginning and when I'm with you
I feel happy
Lets walk for awhile and then we can run
time and our hearts will let us know
if this is love

Keep me in your heart
even when I've hurt you
I need your love most of all
when my frailty is so very obvious
You with your love bind all my wounds
and make me whole again
understanding—tenderness—passionate loyalty
I snuggle in the warmth of your love

You've always let me be—me
that's why I love you
through my small moments
in the sun and my puddles of rain
You've let me be—me
that's why I love you
You've been there for me to lean on
that's why I love you
I'm always trying new things
and you encourage and support me
that's why I love you
I feel free as an eagle and oh so loved

I must travel alone to find my way home
We can be everything to each other
best friends—lovers
I couldn't live without your love
Still;
I must travel alone to find me
the me I know you love
so
I must travel alone to find my way home
home—to you

I was angry
I decided to take a walk in the mountains
The singing mountain creek was like a lullaby
soothing my anger
I stopped to pick wildflowers
of white, yellow, lavender and blue
I soon had a lovely bouquet
their sweet fragrance soothed my anger
I took the path for home
opened the door and gave my love the sweet bouquet
They said it all
I love you—I'm sorry

## Have A Precious Christmas
## Fill It with Love

### A Snowy Cocoon

It's Christmas eve,
We've been housebound all day
because of a prowling blizzard outside.
I feel sort of thankful for this quiet time
just you and I
communicating in our own e.s.p. code
always this closeness
whether I'm in one room knitting and you're
sitting at the kitchen table playing solitaire
or watching our bird friends eating at the feeder
We chat now and then of this and that
but
words aren't really needed between us
the silence speaks a special closeness
You call me to come see what's eating at the birdfeeder
by the tone of your voice I know it's something exciting
My heart quickens its beat, on seeing the dearest present
I could have received on Christmas eve.
A beautiful mourning dove has come out in the blinding
snow storm to wish us a Merry Christmas
The symbol of peace and love
We kiss and embrace in our warm cocoon
It's Christmas

## Have A Precious Christmas
## Fill It With Love

Jesus said it best of all "love one another"

Beacon of Love

A mother and child kneel in prayer
sharing their faith
I drive thru the town and see three new churches
being built to honor Him
Teenage girls clean and polish the elderly couples
home and trim the Christmas tree
their love and kindness warming the house
the ship leaves the harbor carrying medicine, food,
and clothing
Gifts from people with caring hearts to strangers
they will never see
      The wind grew calm and still
      In the stillness a baby cried
      The star lit up the sky
      A beacon for all mankind

Air crisp as ginger snaps
Snow soft as a baby's smile
Snowflakes that dance
to the whispering
gentle wind song
A star shines
like blue crystal
twinkling a message of love

## What Colour Is Love?

I paint pictures with a pen
using pretty coloured words
on a canvas made of paper
My paints—feelings of many hues
Love the blue of my darling's eyes
Faith the whiteness
of a sparkling star
Hope the molten lava red
of the setting sun
knowing it will rise
in the morn
It takes forgiveness
to mend a broken heart
and love to start
its happy beat once again
What colour is forgiveness?
What colour is love?
Only when you've forgiven
someone's wrong
or expressed love
will you know